Rhymes and Verses
of
Edinburgh Town

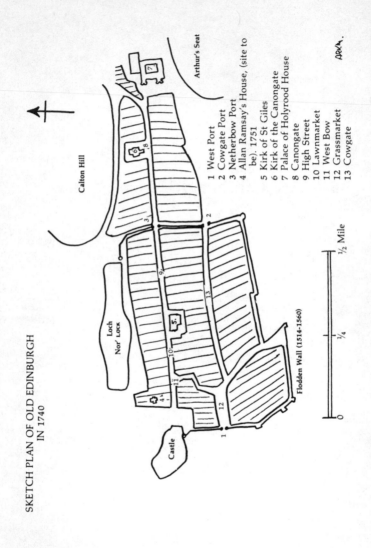

SKETCH PLAN OF OLD EDINBURGH
IN 1740

1 West Port
2 Cowgate Port
3 Netherbow Port
4 Allan Ramsay's House, (site to be). 1751
5 Kirk of St Giles
6 Kirk of the Canongate
7 Palace of Holyrood House
8 Canongate
9 High Street
10 Lawnmarket
11 West Bow
12 Grassmarket
13 Cowgate

Flodden Wall (1514-1560)

Castle

Nor' Loch

Calton Hill

Arthur's Seat

0   ¼   ½ Mile

ARM.

Rhymes and Verses
of
Edinburgh Town

by

ROSS MITCHELL
Illustrations by the Author

Albyn Press Ltd

Made and printed in
Great Britain
and published by
ALBYN PRESS LTD
12 Carlton Terrace
Edinburgh 7
from typesetting by
Alacrity Phototypesetters
Banwell Castle
Weston-Super-Mare

ISBN 0284 98720 4

CONTENTS

INTRODUCTION

THIS BOOK is a celebration in rhymes and verses of the two Edinburghs — the Old Town and the New. It is not a history of Edinburgh, for the subjects chosen — characters, places and events — are neither systematic nor comprehensive. They have been chosen for their interest, but especially for their humour, and for the ways in which they reflect something of the rich life of this capital city, from its beginnings in the mists of the 7th century on Edwin's fortified rock, to the robust architecture and industrial achievements of the late 19th century. The rhymes and verses have been written from the clear and relatively uncomplicated viewpoint of the child, from that of the young man trying to understand the ironies and the contradictions of history, and from that of the adult who delights in the vagaries of human behaviour which have not really changed over all these centuries. The book essentially tells stories about a town and the various folk that have lived in it. The rhymes and verses are arranged in a topographical sequence — beginning in the beginnings with the Castle, proceeding down the Royal Mile to the Palace of Holyrood House, skirting around Arthur's Seat, to return by Sciennes, Greyfriars, Potterrow and the Cowgate; then, as the need for more space led to an urban expansion, the route passes out of the Old Town down the Mound to the New Town and its elegance, beginning in the east with the Calton Hill, passing along Princes Street to the West End, with a final visit to Merchiston and Musselburgh, to end in the foothills of the Pentlands — the Hills of Home.

Because the rhymes and verses must, by their nature, be condensed and full of allusions, they can be fully understood only if their historical context is known. Each is therefore accompanied by a brief annotation which gives the essential facts behind the story. The rhymes and verses are the distillate; the notes are the raw material.

It seemed natural to tell many of the outrageous stories of the Old Town in the vernacular — the language spoken by the people of the time. Because the Lothians (the site of the capital city with its royal residences, and law courts) was early under the domination of the kingdom of Northumbria, this vernacular, as opposed to the Latin spoken by the clerics, grew out of the Anglian tongue of Bede and Caedmon. The local people shaped it to their own purposes, and called it *Inglis*, the language used in the 14th century by John Barbour in his "The Brus", and Andrew of Wyntoun in his "Orygynal Cronykil". Further additions led to its being called *Scottis* and used in the 15th century by Gavin Douglas in his "Aeneid", Robert Henryson in his "Testament of Cressid", and Sir David Lyndsay of the Mount in his "Satire of the Thrie Estatis". Finally, with Scotland's links with the Continent, there were French, Dutch and Germanic additions to what became known as *Lallans* — the common language of the Lowlands, as opposed to the Gaelic of the Highlands. This Lallans was spoken by servant and master alike. It was the spoken tongue of the Scottish Justiciary in the 18th century, at the very time the Lords of Session were writing in the most elegant of English, in deference to the Court in distant London. This Lallans is the rich language of Robert Burns and his predecessor Robert Fergusson. It has been taken up in turn and developed in the present century by poets such as Hugh McDiarmid, William Landles and Douglas Fraser. It is both musical and humorous, but capable of giving a pithy bite to a telling phrase. It is more serviceable than English when we wish to poke gentle fun at our worthy ancestors, as well as laugh at ourselves in the face of our pretensions. When we wish to be serious, or to mimic the elegance of the classic style and aspirations of James Craig's New Town, then English serves us better. In a sense, the two languages represent in themselves the very real differences of the two Edinburghs, differences which are important because they reflect different times, different political pressures and different social needs. But underneath all this continues to pass a cavalcade of the mass of ordinary people, as well as the eccentrics and aristocrats, who are woven into the fabric of the stories.

Dedication to Edinburgh Town

Fair Edina, pride of heaven,
Built on hillsides numbering seven
Like ancient Rome, or more like Athens,
Is just historic as it happens.

Full of tales of the uncanny —
Ghost and witch in every crannie;
Gentlefolk of high renown
Bringing honour to the town.

Surge of battle, clash of wits,
Rival factions, legal writs;
The stuff of stories, high romance,
Lies all around at every glance.

Fair Edina, grant us grace
To recognise your rightful place,
Through these rhymes and verses too,
Dedicated here to you.

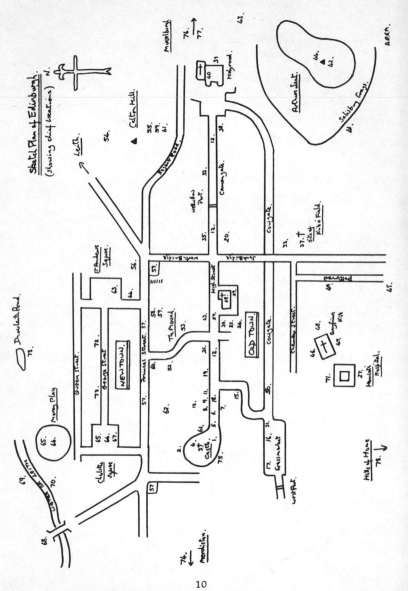

Sketch Plan of Edinburgh.
(showing chief locations)

N.

Drumsheugh Road.
73.

Leith.

Murray Place
Register House

Charlotte Square
65.
66.

George St.
Queen Street.
73.

St Andrews Square
63.
64.

69. 8 70. Water of Leith

NEW TOWN

65.
66.
67.

62.

2.
St Giles
64.
3.
1.
5.

Princes Street. 57.
The Mound.
60.
52.
53.
57.

10.
8, 9, 11.
5. 6. 16.
7.
19.
21.
22.
12.

North Bridge
South Bridge
High Street
23.
37.
24.
25.
28.
32.
34.

57.

56.

54.

Calton Hill
55.
59.
61.

Waterloo Place

Water of Leith

35.
12.
20.

OLD TOWN

15.
30.
Cowgate.
Cowgate
33.
37.
Site of Kirk o Field

Canongate.
33.

Abbeyhill

40.
31.
Holyrood

railway
5.
45.

17. 16. 31.
Grassmarket
West Port.

Chambers Street.
46.
48.
Greyfriars Kk.
47.
71.
27.
Heriot's
Hospital

Arthur Seat
44.
42.

N. Salisbury Crags.
W.

Abbey

Milk of Hope
74.

76. Portobello.

76. Morningside.

10

RHYMES AND VERSES

Edinburgh Castle
and Ross Fountain.

ARKM.

1 Edinburgh Castle

Edinburgh Castle, fine and fair,
Its feet in the rock, its head in the air,
Guarding the city with might and with main
Repulses the enemy, again and again.

Edinburgh Castle, fine and fair,
Its feet in the rock, its head in the air;
Edinburgh Castle, with towering walls,
If ever it's taken, the city falls.

Edinburgh Castle, tall and straight,
Stands above the city gate,
Keeping guard upon the town,
The brightest jewel in its crown.

EDINBURGH CASTLE sits at 437 feet above sea level on top of a rock of volcanic basalt. The earliest building on the site was the castle of Edwin, King of Northumbria (around 629 AD.) When Malcolm II defeated the Northumbrians at the battle of Carham in 1018, the castle became Scottish territory, and has remained so ever since. David I made it his permanent residence in 1124, and then it underwent a series of rebuildings and development during the reigns of Edward III and David II. The present Palace buildings in the SE corner were erected by Mary, Queen of Scots, and here her son James VI was born in 1556. The Castle was under siege from 1567 till 1573 when King David's Tower was replaced with the Half-moon Battery by the Regent Morton. The Castle was remodelled once more in 1651 when the Crown Room was built. It was here in 1818 the Honours of Scotland (the Royal Regalia) were found in a chest. The last major building was that of the National War Memorial to the design of Sir Robert Lorimer, raised on the highest part of the rock in 1927. The Castle has been the setting for much of Edinburgh's turbulent history, both defending it and being attacked itself.

13

2 Sir Thomas Randolph

"Oh gay Sir Thomas Randolph, whit gars ye weep?
Ye hae taen the Castle, and its massy keep;
'Twas William Frank who showed you the path he used
  to climb
When he went a-courtin' his love o' former time."

"O gay Sir Thomas Randolph, why dae ye weep?
For ye've taen the Castle, and its massy keep!"
"I took it for king Robert Bruce, wi' only thirty men,
But I leave it bare and broken, lest it be taen again."

SIR THOMAS RANDOLPH: The Castle was held by troops of Edward
II during the Wars of Independence between Scotland and
England. Sir Thomas Randolph of Strathdon, the Earl of Moray
and nephew of King Robert the Bruce, recaptured the Castle from
the English garrison on the evening of 14th March, 1314. He had
been shown a route up the precipitous castle rock by a William
Frank, who had been stationed in the Castle previously, and had
used this secret route to visit his sweetheart in the town. Sir
Thomas took the Castle with a small band of thirty men, and
destroyed most of the buildings, with the exception of St
Margaret's Chapel, to keep them out of the hands of the English
once more.

3 *St Margaret's Chapel*

Margaret, Malcolm's saintly queen,
Prayed every day to God;
Such saintly virtue every day
Her husband found a rod.

He ordered to be built a kirk
Upon the castle rock,
An' gied it to her for her work,
So none at her might mock.

There, every day, both nicht an' morn,
She prayed upon her knees
That God might note the king forlorn
An' bring him holy ease.

This tiny chapel still does stand
High up for a' tae view,
The auldest kirk in a' the land –
St Margaret's gift in feu.

Chancel Arch,
St Margaret's chapel.
AJKM.

ST MARGARET'S CHAPEL is one of the very few remaining Norman style chapels still to be seen in Scotland. It stands high up on the Castle rock. Margaret, the daughter of the Saxon Edward Atheling, and grand niece of Edward the Confessor, married Malcolm Canmore, who reigned as Malcolm III from 1057 till 1093. Margaret came to Scotland in 1068 to escape from William the Conqueror, accompanied by her Hungarian mother, her sister and brother Edgar. She was a very devout woman who brought Christian learning and culture to the Scottish court. Turgot her Confessor and Saxon Bishop of St Andrews, records in her biography her devotions and works of charity to the poor. Sadly, Malcolm and her son Edward were both killed at Alnwick, just over the border in England. Margaret died of grief, aged only 47, three days later, on 16th November, 1093, and her body was laid in her chapel built for her by her husband, until her body was taken across the River Forth to be buried at Dunfermline. In recognition of her devoted and pious life, she was canonised in 1250 on the recommendation of her well-loved reputation. Over the years her chapel fell into disrepair, but it was restored in 1857 by Queen Victoria.

St Margaret's chapel.
ARKM.

4 Mons Meg

Mons Meg wi' muckle mou'
Fires a cannonball or two;
Gars thae sodgers rise and run,
Here's anither victory won.

Mons Meg wi' muckle mou'
Fires a cannonball or two;
Muckle stanes, wi' fierce intent,
In castle walls mak muckle dent.

MONS MEG is a huge cannon which stands on the Castle ramparts facing north, quite close to St Margaret's chapel. Its origins are obscure, but it may have been forged by a smith called McKim in the first half of the 15th century. As a reward legend says he was given the lands of Mollance in Galloway, and the cannon was named after his wife Margaret — Mollance Meg. James II certainly took the cannon with him to the siege of Threave Castle in Galloway in 1455. The cannon weighs 6½ tons, and could fire a cannonball up to a range of 2 miles. In 1682 it burst firing a salute to the Duke of York (later James II and VII), during his visit to Edinburgh as Commissioner for his brother, Charles II. It was later removed to the armoury in the Tower of London, in 1754, whence it was returned to Edinburgh in 1829 by the efforts of Sir Walter Scott.

5 *Wallace and Bruce*
(Sir William Wallace and King Robert the Bruce)

Wallace on the one side, and Bruce on the other,
Both stand there very still in every kind of weather;
The drawbridge across the moat, they guard so very
well,
But what each is thinking, there's no one can tell.

WALLACE AND BRUCE: Two fine statues to Scotland's leaders in the Wars of Independence — Sir William Wallace and Robert the Bruce, were erected in niches on either side of the main entrance across the moat into the Castle in 1929 to mark the six hundred year anniversary of the Royal Charter given to the town in 1329 by Robert the Bruce.

6 *Nova Scotia*

When lively lords go digging
With sasine on their mind,
'Tis Nova Scotian charters
They're hoping for to find.

When lively lords go digging
Right here in this dark ground,
King Charlie has decreed it
Their charters they have found.

NOVA SCOTIA was discovered in 1497 by John Cabot. It was colonised by the French in 1604, and given the name Arcadia. During the reign of Charles II, the Earl of Stirling obtained permission to colonise the territory in the name of Nova Scotia (New Scotland), and to sell baronetcies to 200 proposed colonists, each of whom had to dig a portion of the land to establish his claim. To save the journey involved, and to encourage colonists, Charles decreed by royal mandate that the soil of the Spur in front of the Castle should be considered Nova Scotian for the purpose of sasine — the document in Scots law which proved legal possession. Sixty-four such baronets availed themselves of the privilege between 1625 and 1649. The territory was disputed with the French, but the British finally took over in 1763. The Spur of land immediately in front of the Castle was replaced by a spacious Esplanade built up from the soil excavated from the foundations of John Adam's Royal Exchange of 1753, and currently the City Chambers, further east from the Castle in the High Street.

7 *Cannonba' Hoose*

"Kin ye see yon cannonba'
Hauf-way up this wa'?"
"Cam it frae yon castle guns?"
"Nae, not at a'."

"It merks the heicht the waters rose
In thon reservoir,
That cam in leaden pipes fu' close
Frae Comiston afar."

CANNONBALL HOUSE was built in 1630 at the top of Castlehill, and saw the castle sieges of 1650, 1689 and 1745. One story says that the cannonball lodged in the side of the house during the siege of 1745. On the other hand, in 1674 a contract worth £50 was given to Peter Brusche, a German engineer, to bring water from wells at Comiston in the Pentland Hills, by means of 3 inch lead pipes to a reservoir at the head of Castlehill, whence it was taken in smaller pipes to 10 cisterns or wells scattered about the Old Town of which one survives outside John Knox's House in the High Street. Brusche is said to have put the lump of lead on the wall of the house to show the height of the wells at Comiston from which the water was drawn.

8 *The Execution Site*

Many a witch her days has ended,
Worrit at the stake;
For crimes committed here are mended,
With fire, and rope and rake.

And high born lords for treason done,
Are brought to trial and death,
And here beneath their last day's sun,
They pay with life and breath.

EXECUTION SITE: Executions took place at the east end of the present Castle Esplanade at the top of Castlehill. Some 2000 executions took place between 1437 and 1670 (James II till Charles II). In 1538, during the reign of James V, the Master of Forbes was executed, followed by Lady Jane Douglas, the widow of John, Lord Glammis, who was said to have attempted to poison the king. Then in 1539, Thomas Forret, vicar of Dollar, John Keiller and John Beveridge — both Blackfriars, Duncan Simpson, priest, and Robert Forrester, Gent., were all executed for heresy. In 1590 and 1591 many witches were burned here, and are commemorated in a plaque and small fountain at the north-east end of the Esplanade. A further 5 witches were burned here in 1659.

9 The Ragged School

Doctor Guthrie's Ragged School
Stood by Castlehill,
Built for urchins, orphans too –
Ragged Jack and Jill.

Jack and Jill crept up the Hill
To get their daily schooling;
Jack and Jill ran down the Hill,
Sent home for cheek and fooling.

THE RAGGED SCHOOL: The Rev Dr Thomas Guthrie, minister of
Old Greyfriars and then St John's, in his "Plea for Ragged
Schools" of 1847, drew attention to the plight of the homeless and
neglected children who at that time wandered the city streets. As
a result of his appeal, he was able to open the Original Ragged
Industrial School in Ramsay Lane off Castlehill that year, and
then other schools elsewhere in the town. These schools took
destitute children of 5 to 14 years who had to be natives of
Edinburgh, or to have lived there for 12 months prior to
application for entry. They were given food, taught reading,
writing, and arithmetic. If they were old enough they were also
taught the rudiments of a craft or trade.

10 *Goose-Pie Hoose*

Allan Ramsay, snug an' warm,
In yer Goose-Pie Hoose;
Ye'll nae come tae ony hairm,
Sittin' thair, richt douce.

GOOSE-PIE HOOSE: Allan Ramsay (1685-1758), Scots poet and leader of the vernacular revival, was the author of "The Gentle Shepherd" — a typical 18th century pastoral epic. In 1725 he began the first circulating library in the city, from a booth in the High Street. In 1751 he commissioned a house to be built on a prime site, now by Ramsay Gardens overlooking the Nor' Loch. A contemporary wag likened it to a goose pie, with Allan sitting warm like a goose within it. A statue of him by Sir John Steell was erected in 1867 at the entrance to West Princes Street Gardens.

11 *The Camera Obscura*

A camera obscura rare
Sits on Geddes' dark tower there,
Projecting scenes on table white
To give the viewers pure delight;

Living colours from without,
Brought by periscope no doubt
Into the shadows of that room –
Woven light upon a loom;

A tapestry of moving shades,
Miniatures of a life that fades
When the door is opened wide –
And the real world steps inside.

Outlook Tower.

mkh.

THE CAMERA OBSCURA: In 1846 Maria Theresa Short's observatory was built into a 17th century building on Castlehill, thus to be known as the Outlook Tower. She devised a camera obscura, literally "shadowy room" — a device whereby coloured and moving images of the outside world could be projected onto a circular white table in a darkened chamber. This was installed in the Outlook Tower in 1855, and created quite a sensation for its novelty. Then in 1891, Patrick Geddes (1854-1932) a pioneer in sociology and town planning acquired the Outlook Tower, and redeveloped the group of houses close by, now known as Ramsay Gardens. The Outlook Tower with its camera obscura still in working order, was sold to Edinburgh University in the 1950s.

12 The Royal Mile

The Royal Mile gangs up an' doon,
The muckle back-bane o' the toun;
Frae Castle high tae Palace low,
See the bonnie sodgers go.

Frae Castlehill tae auld Tron Kirk
Hear "Gardyloo!" cried i' the mirk,
While debtors in the Tolbooth clink
Hae plenty time tae sit an' think.
"Saint Giles Kirk, wi' massy croun,
Bless the folk that pass at noon!"
By the luckenbooths an' stalls,
By closes, wynds, Assembly Halls,
On past fiery Knox's hoose –
"Wheest, nae soun' frae man nor moose!"
Doon tae Canongate and Kirk
Where awfu' frichtsome ghaisties lurk,
On tae White Horse Close for brandy –
"If ony's feart, it comes in handy!"
Tae find at last by Abbey Strand
Sanctuary, and the Palace grand.

The Royal Mile gangs up an' doon,
The muckle back-bane o' the toun;
Frae Castle high tae Palace low,
See the merchin' sodgers go.

THE ROYAL MILE is the thoroughfare, just over a mile in length, that runs down the ridge from the Castle rock to the Palace of Holyrood. It is made up of Castlehill, the Lawnmarket, the High Street, the Canongate and the Abbey Strand.

TRON KIRK built in 1643 to a design of John Mylne at the site of the old public weigh beam (tron). Gutted by fire in 1824. New spire built in 1828. Closed for public worship in 1952.

Knox's House,
High Street.

TOLBOOTH: in 1386 the building where tolls were paid. Became prison for debtors in 1480. Used as a general prison by 1640. First used for public hangings in 1785. Demolished in 1817.

ST GILES KIRK: High Kirk of St Giles dedicated in 1243 by the Bishop of St Andrews. Burned by troops of Richard II in 1385. Rebuilt, and became Collegiate Church in 1466. The Lantern Tower (the Crown) was added around 1500. John Knox preached for first time in 1559.

LUCKENBOOTHS: closed or lockable shops of the 15th century. They were demolished in 1817, like the Tolbooth, in a street widening scheme.

CLOSE: private passage, open by day, but closed at night.

WYND: public thoroughfare, always open from end to end.

ASSEMBLY HALLS: various to be found in Lawnmarket, High Street and West Bow.

JOHN KNOX (1505-1572) Scottish Protestant preacher and leader of the Scottish Reformation in 1538. Said to have lived for a time in a 16th century house still surviving in the High Street.

CANONGATE: street of the Canons of Holyrood Abbey. Kirk built in 1688 for the displaced congregation of the Abbey

Canongate Tolbooth.

Church at Holyrood, when James II made it the Chapel of the Knights of the Thistle.

WHITE HORSE CLOSE: site of the White Horse Inn of 1623, from where travellers set out by stage coach to London.

ABBEY STRAND between the Canongate and Holyrood Palace, marks the limit of sanctuary for all kinds of crime until 1560, when it applied only to crimes of debt thereafter.

White Horse Close.

13 *The Pipes beneath your Feet*

Softly, softly as you go –
He plays below the street;
Hush, do you hear them sound,
The pipes beneath your feet?

Softly, softly as you go –
He walks his ghostly beat;
Hush, do you hear them sound,
The pipes beneath your feet?

Softly, softly as you go –
The route he must complete;
Hush, do you hear them now,
The pipes beneath your feet?

THE PIPES BENEATH YOUR FEET: a story goes that once upon a time there was a passageway running beneath the Royal Mile, all the way from the Castle on its rock, down to the Palace of Holyrood. A piper volunteered to test out the passage. He would march down the tunnel playing his pipes so that people above could judge his progress. All went well until about half-way down, when suddenly the pipes were heard to stop in mid breath, and the piper was never again seen on earth after that day. However, it is said that if you listen carefully, you may hear his ghostly pipes sounding out beneath your feet as you pass down the Royal Mile.

14　*The Countess of Argyll*

The Countess of Argyll she goes
In weather foul and fair,
Up the hill and down the hill,
In her sedan chair.

THE COUNTESS OF ARGYLL: in the mid 17th century, the then Countess of Argyll caused a mild sensation by being carried by two burly Highland retainers in a sedan chair, up and down the Royal Mile. She was being taken, whatever the weather, to visit her husband the Marquis, who had been imprisoned in the Castle by Charles II, for collaborating with Cromwell's government. The sedan chair became a fashionable means of travel, the first licence to place chairs for hire being granted by the magistrates in 1687. Most of the chair-men were stalwart highlanders, necessary to carry their hire up and down the steep streets of the Town. The last sedan chair disappeared from the City in the late 1850s.

15 *Major Thomas Weir*

It fell aboot the Lammas tide
When nichts were lang an' mirk,
That Major Weir, yon warlock dread
Stepped oot tae dae his work.

By day he was a prayerfu' man;
At nicht he served the Deil –
He summoned daemons frae the earth,
Gart bogles daunce a reel.

He kept a much carved thornwood staff –
The wonder o' the world;
It rose wi' grace an' drew the door,
When'er the pin was tirled.

It went his errands on command;
It shoppit in the Bow;
It acted as his link-boy when
By dark he had to go.

His sister Grizel kenn'd the airts,
An' she could spin an' sew;
She had the power tae conjure spells
Tae cast on freend or foe.

Folk saw him an' his sister skulk
Aboot the Toun at nicht,
In some great black an' spectral coach –
It gied them a' a fricht.

At last the twa maun pay the price
For a' their Devil's play –
They burnt him on the Gallow Hill,
An' hangit her next day.

Now folk declare they've seen them since
Pass up an' doon the Bow,
Wi' hideous sichts an' awfu' shrieks –
'Tis thus such legends grow.

MAJOR THOMAS WEIR was born of good family in Lanarkshire in 1599. He enlisted in the Regiment of the Earl of Lanark, and rose to the rank of Major. In 1641 he was sent with the Covenantors troops to put down the Irish Papists in Ulster. By 1649 he had returned to Scotland as the commander of the Edinburgh City Guard, and was in charge of the escort that took the Marquis of Montrose to his execution in 1650. Known as Angelical Thomas, he was a strict Presbyterian, with a reputation as a formidable preacher. He lived with his sister Grizel in a house at the Head of the West Bow, and they were members of the group known as the Bowhead Saints. At the age of 71, he fell seriously ill and confessed freely to all kinds of incest, bestiality and wizardry, in conjunction with his sister. She appears to have been even more disturbed because it was she who described her brother's pact with the Devil, and spread the tale that he had a thornwood staff that ran his errands, and opened the door when visitors called. On the strength of these confessions they were brought to trial on 9th April, 1670, and were convicted of charges of incest, adultery and bestiality. The charges of witchcraft were taken for granted. Weir was strangled and then burned along with his staff at the Gallow Hill, mid way between Edinburgh and Leith on the site of present day Greenside Church, and Grizel was hanged at the Grassmarket next day. For the next hundred years their house in the Bow was said to be haunted and the last attempt by a William Patullo and his family to live in the house around 1818 came to a dramatic end after a terrifying night of hauntings and fearful apparitions. The house was finally demolished in 1878 to make way for new buildings at the Head of the Bow.

16 *Maggie Dickson*

Maggie Dickson killed her child,
An' for that was hangit;
They laid her in a buryin' kist
Upon a cairt that clankit.

Cairt an' a' yanked doon the brae,
O'er the highway cobbles;
In the kist the corp lay close,
Jouked aboot wi' wobbles.

Wi' a' the shooglin' she revived,
Unco hale an' hairty;
An' lang syne, she's aye been kenn'd
As Half-Hangit Maggie.

MAGGIE DICKSON was born in Inveresk, near Musselburgh, and in her time became a High Street fish-wife. Later she worked in an inn at Kelso. She was abandoned by her husband in 1723, and then had an illegitimate child which died soon after birth in uncertain circumstances. She hid the body in the long grass by the side of the River Tweed where it was ultimately found. She was charged under the Concealment of Pregnancy Act of 1690, and was hanged on the 2nd of September, 1724. Her body was put in a coffin on a cart which was bumped down the High Street on its way to burial at Inveresk. Halfway there her friends stopped for refreshment at an inn in Peffermill. Groans were heard coming from the coffin, and she was found to be still alive inside. It was held that as the sentence had been carried out, she could not be tried again. She lived on for a further 40 years, and was always known as "Half-Hangit Maggie".

17 Burke and Hare

Burke and Hare went roond the toun
Tae see wha they micht smother;
They found some sixteen vagrant folk,
Consigned them a'taegither.

The corps were sent tae Surgeons' Square,
For Doctors a' maun practise,
But ane o' them was known, an' so
Thae twa were brocht tae justice.

*   *   *

"Burke an' Hare, are ye there,
Sneekin' bodies doon the stair?
Hare an' Burke, in the mirk,
Are ye at yer dreadfu' work?
Bodies snatched for Doctor Knox –
Curses on ye, plague an' pox."

Burke and Hare's House.
Tanner's Close.
1828.

BURKE AND HARE, two Ulster Catholics, came to Scotland around 1818 as itinerant labourers to work on the Union Canal. Burke, with his girl friend, Helen McDougal, set up in a lodging house with Hare and his wife in Tanner's Close in the West Port district. Robert Knox, a distinguished anatomist was running a rival medical school in Surgeons' Square, and with 400 students, badly needed bodies for dissection. When an old pensioner named Donald died, owing them his rent, Burke and Hare sold his body to Dr Knox for £10. When other lodgers were seen to be ailing, they conceived the idea of helping them on their way by smothering them, so that the cause of death would not be obvious, and in turn sold these bodies to Knox and his assistants. So lucrative was this trade that in all they killed off some 16 people, many vagrants whom no one would miss. Unfortunately, one of these was Mary Paterson, a young prostitute known to some of Knox's students, and with this and charges laid against them by a couple named Gray who lived in the same lodging house, Burke and Hare were charged with murder. Despite popular belief, they were never resurrectionists, that is obtaining the bodies by robbing recent burials. Hare was persuaded to turn King's Evidence and he and his wife were set free. Thus in the end, despite mob fury, Burke and McDougal were charged on 8th December, 1828 with the murders. In the end, the case against McDougal was Not Proven, and Burke alone paid the penalty by being hung before a crowd of 25,000 on the 28th January, 1829. His body was dissected, and his skeleton is preserved in the Anatomy Department, the oldest Irish inhabitant of Edinburgh University!

Thomas Gledstanes Land.
Lawnmarket.
17°c.

18 *A Lawnmarket Lullaby*

"Wheesht, ma bairnie, dinna girn,
Sune yer faither will return;
A' the warld's a whigmaleerie,
Turnin' roun' an' tapsalteerie.

Wheesht, ma bairnie, dinna greet,
I see yer faither in the street;
A' the warld's a whigmaleerie,
Turnin' roun' an' tapsalteerie."

A LAWNMARKET LULLABY sung in one of the tall tenements, such
as Thomas Gledstane's Land (now the property of the National
Trust), in the Lawnmarket, by a mother trying to get her child off
to sleep. It is a nonsense rhyme, in which the sense of the words is
less important than the music of their continued and repeated
use.

Eleanor Campbell, the late Lady Stair,
Married Lord Primrose who brought her despair;
His Lordship abroad, tried to marry another –
But the truth was revealed in a magic mirror.

Eleanor Campbell, the late Lady Stair,
Enquired of her brother, who had been there,
Just what had happened, His Lordship's intent;
He confirmed that the mirror had previewed the event.

Eleanor Campbell, the late Lady Stair,
Vowed to wed no man, wealthy or fair;
But wooed by the Earl who then gave her his name,
She out-lived him by twelve years, that lady of fame.

COUNTESS LADY STAIR: Eleanor Campbell, the granddaughter of the Earl of Loudon, the Chancellor of Scotland, married James, Viscount Primrose, in her youth. He was so cruel and violent towards her that she had to escape from him, and he then went to live abroad. A fortune teller came to Edinburgh, claiming to have a magic mirror. Lady Primrose consulted him over the whereabouts of her errant husband, and she saw in the mirror her husband about to marry a young woman. A figure resembling her own brother rushed in to stop the bigamous marriage and the scene in the mirror faded. Her brother returned to Edinburgh some time afterwards, and told his sister what had happened, exactly as seen by her in the mirror. Lord Primrose died in 1706, and she declared that she would never marry again, but was successfully wooed by the Earl of Stair. Together, they became noted figures in the social life of Edinburgh in the mid 18th century. She died in 1759, having survived her second husband by twelve years. Sir Walter Scott used the incident of the fortune teller in his story "My Aunt Margaret's magic mirror". Lady Stair's House is now one of the City museums, containing relics of Robert Burns and Walter Scott.

20 *"Cleanse the Causeway"*

Hamiltons and Douglases are met in an affray,
Hamiltons and Douglases will fight it out today.

Earl of Arran, Earl of Angus, in Blackfriars Wynd,
Each shall fight the other till the victory's assigned.

Hamiltons and Douglases are met in an affray,
Douglases and Angus shall, by arms, prevail this day.

CLEANSE THE CAUSEWAY: in April, 1520, in the neighbourhood of
Blackfriars Wynd, a street brawl broke out between the Hamiltons, the supporters of the Earl of Arran (grandson of James II),
and the Douglases, supporters of the Earl of Angus (husband to
the widow of James IV). The brawl lasted all day, but in the end
the Douglases routed the Hamiltons, and won the skirmish. The
affray was popularly known as "Cleanse the Causeway".

Up the hill, and down the hill
The busy people go,
Caught up in their daily tasks,
Passing to and fro.

Gentlemen, and Ladies too,
Out to take the air;
Ragamuffins of the town,
With dirty legs all bare.

Chairmen, and young Caddies wait,
Touting for their hire;
Advocates in wigs and gowns,
Judges in the mire.

Soldiers marching in close ranks
Down the Royal Mile;
Lovers coyly holding hands,
See it all and smile.

STREET SCENE: a depiction of the busy life of the main thorough-fare of the old town. There is a great contrast between the elegant ladies and gentlemen of fashion, and the hordes of urchins and derelict children. The chairmen, mostly Highland retainers, carry the sedan chairs of the wealthy, and the caddies, a corps of messengers are ready to ply their trade anywhere between Castlehill and Canongate. In the area around Parliament Square, the advocates and judges in their legal robes are a common sight, as are the platoons of soldiers doing duty between the Castle and the Palace of Holyrood.

Lord Monboddo holds it true
That babes are born with tails;
Whenever one is close he peers,
Though each inspection fails.

A pig pursues Lord Gardenstone,
And follows him about;
It sleeps upon his bed at night
And keeps the cold wind out.

TWO LORDS OF SESSION: Edinburgh in the mid 18th century was at the height of the Scottish Enlightenment, and a major part in this was played by the legal profession. The Lords of Session, the King's Judges, were placed in the top rank of citizens in the Edinburgh Directory of 1773-4, followed by Advocates, Writers to the Signet, and only then by physicians and noblemen. Among the Lords of Session were many men of letters such as Henry Home, Lord Kames, and Sir David Dalrymple, Lord Hailes. Although they showed an elegant formality in their writings, they were coarse in their speech. They also counted in their numbers some marked eccentrics.

LORD MONBODDO (James Burnett), caricatured as "an old stuffed monkey in Judges' robes", anticipated Darwin by holding that human babies were born with tails. He kept trying to prove his theory by natural observation, but singularly failed.

LORD GARDENSTONE (Francis Garden) took a fancy to keeping pigs, and a young one kept following him about wherever he went. When it grew old, he hadn't the heart to have it killed, but let it sleep on his bed at night, claiming that it kept him warm.

23 *Lord Coalstoun's Wig*

Twa wee lassies playin'
Wi' a kitten on a string,
Dangled frae their windae,
Whit a daft-like thing!
  Lord Coalstoun stuck his heid oot
Tae tak the early breeze,
Then saw his ain kenspeckle wig
Rise through the air wi' ease!

LORD COALSTOUN'S WIG : it was the habit of Judges and Advocates
to dress up at home, prior to going out to court. In the tall houses
in the High Street, they would often lean out of the windows both
for a breath of fresh air, and for a gossip, before walking up to the
courts in Parliament Square. Robert Chambers in his *Traditions of
Edinburgh* describes an incident in which Lord Coalstoun, all
bewigged, stuck his head out one morning. Unfortunately, in the
house above him two young girls were playing with a kitten on a
string. The animal caught its claws in his Lordship's wig, and the
girls, seeing what had happened, drew the kitten up on the string,
with the wig attached. All Lord Coalstoun saw was his wig
ascending through the morning air as if by its own power. So
disturbed was he by this unnatural sight, that he forswore strong
claret for some time afterwards!

24 Lord Braxfield

Lord Braxfield was a hangin' judge,
The scourge o' ilka felon:
He dispensed justice in a way
It disna pay tae dwell on.

Each thief an' villain shook wi' dread
When callit up for judgin';
"Ye're guilty richt, an' so ye'll be
Nane the waur o' hangin'!"

LORD BRAXFIELD: Robert MacQueen, Lord of Session in 1776, and Lord Justice Clerk in 1788, took the title of Lord Braxfield. He was reknowned for the harshness of his judgements and the coarseness of his humour. His favourite riposte to defending counsel on their guilty clients was "He'll be nane the waur o' a hangin'!" He sat in judgement, and condemned Deacon Brodie at his trial in 1788. Robert Louis Stevenson is said to have taken him as the model for Weir of Hermiston.

See – "Gardyloo!", the cry gaes oot,
Tak heed where're ye wander;
Sic habits hardly lend themsels'
Tae mak the hairt grow fonder.

For "Gardyloo!" means watch yer step,
Wi' slops slung in the runner;
An' a' the stink, an' a' the mess,
Fair gies us sic a scunner.

So, as ye gang aboot at nicht,
Keep listenin' for the warnin';
Cry – "Haud yer hand!" in plenty time
Gif ye'd keep braw till mornin'.

"GARDYLOO!" derived from 18th century French — "Gare de l'eau." — Look out for the water, was a warning shouted out that slops and household rubbish were about to be thrown out of a window in to the public thoroughfare. This usually took place about 10 o'clock at night, and unless the unwary passersby called out "Haud your hand!" they were liable to be caught in the malodorous deluge. Needless to say, the streets stank from this habit, which was not repressed by the Town Council until 1730.

Now, William Brodie, Guild of Wrights,
Has built new gallows grim;
After a life of work, and crime,
They were reserved for him.

For Deacon Brodie, fine by day,
By night a practised thief,
Had fashioned keys to open doors –
But then, he came to grief.

He broke into the Excise room
In lower Canongate;
When caught his assistants, through fear,
Did all his crimes relate.

Now Deacon Brodie's gone to Hell,
Or where such villains go;
His gallows worked – it was his style
To step both high and low!

DEACON BRODIE: William Brodie, Deacon of the Guild of Wrights (masons and carpenters) designed a new gallows with a mechanical drop to replace the two ladders from one of which the condemned was "pushed off". Brodie had a reputation for uprightness by day, but in the evenings he turned to riotous living. He did not however turn to active crime until the last 7 years of his life. He used his official position to obtain impressions of keys in putty or clay so that he could then easily burgle secure premises. On the evening of 5th March, 1787, he broke into the Excise Office in Chessels Court in the lower Canongate. He was almost caught in the act, but his accomplice Brown (alias Humphrey Moore, an Englishman under threat of transportation) turned King's Evidence, and Brodie was brought to trial, judged guilty by Lord Braxfield, and ironically executed on the gallows of his own design, on the 1st of October, 1788. Attempts were made to resuscitate him afterwards, but to no avail. His double life may have been taken by Robert Louis Stevenson as the basis for his story *Dr Jekyll and Mr Hyde*.

27 *Ginglin' Geordie Heriot*

Ginglin' Geordie, ae guid morrow!
See, King Jamie's come tae borrow
From ye, gold and siller coin;
Gie him wine an' guid sirloin.

Ginglin' Geordie, James' guid Grace
Is come tae gie ye pride o' place;
If ye let him money borrow,
It will bring ye joy, – an' sorrow!

GINGLIN' GEORDIE HERIOT was official jeweller and goldsmith to James VI. He had a tiny shop close by St Giles where the King would often visit him to see his work, but also to borrow money from him, but rarely to pay it back. There is a story that Heriot one day to shame the King, lit a fire in his shop from a bond for two thousand pounds which he had lent James. He followed the King to London where he prospered sufficiently to be able to leave a sum of money for a hospital and educational establishment to be built in his name. This was completed in 1650 on the land just west of Greyfriars Kirkyard.

28 Jenny Geddes

Jenny Geddes in Saint Giles
Objeckit tae the Prayers;
She flung her stool, an' callit oot –
"Nae Mass'll deave ma ears."

Oor Jenny, filled wi' richteous ire
Agin the King's Decree,
Then flung her stool, an' callit oot –
"Ye'll nae say Mass at me."

JENNY GEDDES: Charles I had declared the High Kirk of Saint Giles to be a cathedral, and that the new Episcopal Prayer Book should be used in Scottish worship. In Saint Giles, on the morning of Sunday, the 23rd of July, 1637 when Dean James Hanna was invited by David Lindsay, the first Bishop of Edinburgh, to read the Day's Collect from the new Book of Prayer, Jenny Geddes, a herb-woman, and fervent Presbyterian, took a leading part in the riot that ensued. She is said to have picked up her "creepie", the small folding stool that people were wont to bring with them to sit on before the days of static pews, and flung it at the Dean, crying out "The Deil colic the waim o' ye!" (The Devil give you colic in your stomach!) She is said earlier in the service to have struck a man on the head with her Bible, with the words "Ye daur tae say Mass at ma lug!" (Don't dare say Mass in my ear!), for his temerity in taking part in the Responses.

29 King Charlie's Cuddie

Come tae Parliament Close wi' me,
Charlie's cuddie we maun see
Rearin' on its muckle block.
– Tak ye heed ye dinna mock!

Charlie's cuddie's braw an' frisky,
Tryin' tae ride it could be risky;
Haud it firmly by the heid.
– 'Tis a shame it's made o' leid!

Charlie, man, ye're fine an' dashin',
A' got up in Roman fashion;
Watch it disna throw ye aff.
– 'Sakes, we couldna help but laugh!

KING CHARLIE'S CUDDIE: on the 16th of April, 1685 a lead equestrian statue was erected in Parliament Close, in memory of
Charles II. The King is shown in the garb of an Emperor, without
spurs or stirrups in the Roman style. The whole project cost
£2580 Scots. The ordinary people were amazed at its appearance,
and not quite sure what to make of it. It remains, however, the
oldest equestrian statue made of lead surviving in this country.

30 *Heart o' Midlothian*

Heart o' Midlothian
Drawn there in stone,
Though folk a' walk on ye,
Ye never moan.

Heart o' Midlothian
Why are ye there?
A' the folk spit on ye,
Are ye nae sair?

Heart o' Midlothian
Tolbooth ye mark:
Grim place o' sufferin'
Fearsome an' dark.

Heart o' Midlothian
If ye had tongue,
Whit tales o' olden days
Ye micht hae sung.

HEART O' MIDLOTHIAN was the name given by Sir Walter Scott to the Old Tolbooth in his novel of Edinburgh life of the same name. The site of this forbidding prison, and one time place of execution, is now marked by a heart shape in the cobbles of the High Street, just west of St Giles. There has grown up a tradition of spitting on this heart shape, possibly to express dislike for the grim building it commemorates.

31 *The Porteous Riots*

Captain Porteous – fate awaits ye,
Commander o' the Guard;
For the angry mob's condemned ye,
And ye'll find it hard.

Syne they've sprung ye frae the Tolbooth,
Dragged ye doon the Bow,
Noo they'll hang ye, that's the haill truth,
Glad tae see ye go.

THE PORTEOUS RIOTS: at the hanging in the Grassmarket, on the 16th of April 1736, of Andrew Wilson, a Fife smuggler, the crowd sympathetic to him tried to intervene. Captain Porteous, the then Commander of the Town Guard, fearing a disturbance, ordered his troops to fire on the crowd. Seven people were killed, and Porteous was arrested, charged with murder, and imprisoned in the Tolbooth. On the 7th of September, following a rumour that because of his standing Porteous might be exonerated, the angry mob broke into the Tolbooth, and dragged him down the West Bow into the Grassmarket, to the scene of his crime. There they hanged him from a dyer's pole, with a rope which they had taken from a nearby shop, leaving a guinea behind in payment.

32 The Caddies

Here's the caddie, mark him weel;
He'll tak' ye doon the road.
He kens the way – wi' him ye're safe;
He earns whit he is owed.

He meets his cronies at the Cross,
For clavers an' a crack;
He'll tak yer message whaur ye please,
An' bring anither back.

THE CADDIES from the French — le cadet, meaning junior, were a corps of street messengers. They ran errands, escorted people up and down the maze of streets, carried water from the Town wells, and generally acted as an early form of Town Guard. Like the chairmen who carried the sedan chairs, they used to gather for a chat around the Mercat Cross in the High Street, while waiting for hire.

33 The Shootin' o' the Bailie

Bailie McMorran was call'd tae the Schule
Because of a civil affray;
The lads were in riot, an' makin' a fuss –
A' for a holiday.

The Bailie went up tae the lockit front yett,
An' spak tae their leader, Sinclair –
"Come, open the yetts, an' get back tae yer buiks;
Let's in, an' mak trouble nae mair."

The rowt grew much worse, an' Sinclair wi' his gun
Then shot him point blank in the heid.
The schule lads bide trial in the Canongate jail
Noo Bailie McMorran is deid.

THE SHOOTIN' O' THE BAILIE: Bailie John McMorran was sent on
the 15th of September, 1595, to quell a riot that had broken out at
the High School. This had been built in 1578 in the grounds of the
Blackfriars monastery off the Canongate. The boys were deman-
ding a holiday, and had barricaded themselves in, under the
leadership of William Sinclair, son of the Chancellor of Caithness.
McMorran tried to remonstrate with the boys, but Sinclair finally
shot him. The ringleaders were held in the nearby Canongate
Tolbooth, pending trial for McMorran's murder, but were
released because of Sinclair's connections. This event is recalled
each year by the Royal High School in the reading of the School
Rules which expressly forbid any boy to bring firearms into the
School precincts.

34 *The Maiden*

Thon is a Maiden o' dubious chairms,
See that ye dinna fall into her airms.
Dinna get snuggit, pray mark ma word, Sir;
Aiblins ye'll quick lose yer heid over her.

THE MAIDEN was the nickname given to the Scottish form of
guillotine which was built in Halifax in 1564. It was brought to
Scotland on the recommendation of James Douglas, Earl of
Morton, later to be Regent during the minority of James VI. The
Maiden was used as an instrument of execution, particularly for

noblemen, from 1566 until 1710. Two of its victims were the Regent himself in 1580, and the Marquis of Argyll in 1661.

"The Maiden".

35 *Heave Awa' Hoose*

In Eighteen Hundred and Sixty One
A brave and wondrous thing was done:
A hoose fell doon wi' muckle cloot,
An' they had tae dig a laddie oot.

His voice rose clear – "Noo, dinna fret;
Heave awa' lads, I'm no deid yet!"

HEAVE AWA' HOOSE: a 7 storey tenement, built by Trotter in 1612 on the north side of the High Street, suddenly collapsed early on the morning of Sunday, the 24th of November, 1861. The cries of a young boy from the rubble drew attention to his survival, and as a token of his courage he called out to his rescuers — "Heave awa' lads, I'm no deid yet!" Charles Dickens who was in Edinburgh at the time, visited the scene of the disaster. The building put up in its place commemorates the event with a bust of the young boy above the entrance, together with his immortal words.

36 *The Ladies o' Traquair*

The Ladies o' Traquair sit doon
Tae tak their midday meal,
O' mutton broth, an' peas weel done,
But ne'er the rich man's veal.

The Ladies o' Traquair sit doon
For scones an' tea at Four;
Just leave the saucer wi' its spoon,
Gin ye would wish for more.

THE LADIES O' TRAQUAIR: Ladies Barbara and Margaret Stuart, twin daughters of Charles, the 4th Earl of Traquair, lived as spinster ladies of repute in a house near St Mary's Wynd at the head of the Canongate. Like many of the gentry of that time in the 18th century, their life style though genteel had to be very frugal, as testified by their very simple diet. In such society, in order not to give or take offence, there were elaborate rituals to protect propriety. For example, when taking tea, you left your spoon in the saucer, rather than in the cup, as a signal that you would accept some more if the hostess had not run out of victuals. The last of the two sisters died in 1794.

37 *At Kirk o' Field*

At Kirk o' Field the deed was done
In Fifteen Sixty Seven –
Lord Darnley and his serving man
Blown up, and sent to heaven.

Or so, at first, the crime appeared;
The plot was badly mangled –
Examination of them showed
Both dead, but each was strangled.

AT KIRK O' FIELD: the house of the Provost of Kirk o' Field (Church of St Mary in the Fields) was built close to the old town walls on the south side of both the Canongate and Cowgate. Here, on the evening of the 9th/10th February, 1567 Henry, Lord Darnley the King Consort to Mary, Queen of Scots, and his servant man were killed in an explosion. On closer inspection each was found to have been strangled prior to the explosion. This gave rise to the suspicion of a conspiracy of the Scottish Lords, including James Hepburn, Earl of Bothwell, to murder Darnley and thus release Mary from her continuing marriage to Darnley. That there was a conspiracy there is no doubt; what remains uncertain, is whether the deed was done with Mary's knowledge or not.

38 *The Monster of Queensberry House*

The heir to Drumlanrig was left on his own,
And down to the kitchen went he;
He found a young lad working there all alone,
So he killed him, and cooked him for tea.

THE MONSTER OF QUEENSBERRY HOUSE: the heir to Drumlanrig, the eldest son of James, second Duke of Queensberry, was a congenital idiot of great physical strength. He was kept in a downstairs room in Queensberry House at the foot of the Canongate. On the day in 1707 when the Union with England was passed, the family left him alone in the house. Sadly, he got out and wandered down to the kitchens, where he found a young serving lad preparing a meal. He killed the boy and ate up all the food he could find. When the Duke's party returned to the house, they found him roasting the body of the kitchen lad on one of the kitchen spits.

The King sat in his castle old
Thinkin' whit he micht dae –
"O whaur will I get an architect
Tae build a palace gay?"

Then up an' spak an ancient wight
Wha kenned a thing or two –
"Leonard Logie's the architect
Will dae the job for you."

The King commanded word be sent
Tae set the project doon,
An' Maister Logie gat the task
Tae build this palace soon.

He seekit for a proper site,
An' searchit a' he could;
He found spare land – "We'll build it here,
Near Kirk o' Holy Rood."

An' noo the King sits snug an' warm
Inside his palace grand,
"Aye, Holyrood's a braw, braw hoose,
The finest in my land."

THE PALACE O' HOLYROOD HOOSE: the Abbey of the Holy Rood, with its precious remnant of the True Cross, was founded by David I in 1128, and built on land at the foot of the Canongate, under the shelter of the hill, Arthur's Seat. When Edinburgh Castle became too austere for the Royal Household, James IV began in 1498 plans to build a Palace to be known as Holyrood

Palace of Holyrood House.

DRKM.

House, on the land adjacent to the Abbey. On the 10th of September, 1504, a Master Logy or Logie was paid £40 for the plans he had submitted. The original building was enlarged in 1515 by James V, and repaired in 1561 after the damage sustained in Lord Hertford's raids of 1544 and 1547 (Henry VIII's Rough Wooing of Scotland). It was partly rebuilt for Cromwell, the Lord Protector, in 1658. The modern palace of today was reconstructed, on the orders of Charles II, in 1671 by the Royal Mason Robert Mylne, to a design of Sir William Bruce.

Italian Davie played the lute
For Mary, Scotland's queen,
But Scottish lordlings took offence
At what this act might mean.

Poor Davie and the Queen ignored
The warnings they were given;
He was despatched before her eyes,
And straightway sent to heaven.

They struck him down with swords and dirks,
So he should play no more;
Today, they'll show you Davie's blood
Fresh, on the Palace floor!

DAVIE RICCIO: David Riccio, a Catholic from Savoy, the border-
land between Italy and France, came to Scotland in 1561 to be a
Valet of the Bedchamber to Mary, Queen of Scots. In 1564 he was
appointed as her Secretary, and acted as companion to the
unfortunate Lord Darnley, Mary's second husband. Davie was of
small stature and hunch-backed, yet he dressed in a very ornate
and rather dandyish way. This and his Catholic faith did not
endear him to the Scots. But he was a fine musician and became
the confidant of the Queen. There were even rumours that he
was her lover. On the evening of Saturday, the 9th of March,
1566, he was with the now pregnant Queen in her Supper Room
on the second floor of the north-west corner of the old palace. A
group of Scots Lords burst in on the Queen and dragged Davie
from her skirts. They killed him in front of her by 50 to 60 stab
wounds. Until recent times visitors to that part of the Palace were
shown fresh blood on the wooden floor, said to be that of Riccio!
The spot is now marked by a brass plaque.

41 *The Radical Runner*

Round and round the Radical Road
The radical rascal ran;
Back and forth by Salisbury Crags
To run as fast as he can.

THE RADICAL RUNNER: Arthur's Seat, 822 feet above sea level, is
an extinct volcanic plug. The name may come from King Arthur,
but more likely from the Gaelic-Ard na Saigheid, meaning
"Height of the Arrows". Salisbury Crags, a prominent feature on
the west side, are formed by an uptilted volcanic plate. That name
is probably from the Anglo Saxon — Saer burh —"dry place". In
1820 the Radical Road was built round the base of the Crags to
give work to the unemployed of the time.

42 *The Crouchin' Lion*

Whit dae ye see when ye squint at yon hill?
Is it a lion, sittin' sae still?
Is it some beastie that we kin a' share?
Or jist a hillock, hunkered doon there?

THE CROUCHIN' LION: from certain directions, Salisbury Crags,
the Summit and the Whinny Hill parts of Arthur's Seat, take on
the aspect of a crouching lion. An oriental visitor to the City saw
the Summit more as an elephant's head. Some people see one
thing, others just the hill itself, a very prominent feature of the
Capital's skyline.

43 Muschat's Cairn

Nicol Muschat had a wife,
Her maiden name was Hall;
He cut her throat from ear to ear,
And left her by the wall.

Nicol Muschat had a wife,
But soon grew tired of her;
A surgeon trained, he used a knife
As records do aver.

He took her for a walk one night,
And in the Park they paused;
He cut her throat down to the bone,
And thus her death he caused.

When brought to trial he confessed all,
And guilty, he was hung,
A cairn was raised to mark the spot
Where his foul deed was done.

MUSCHAT'S CAIRN: Nicol Muschat, a young surgeon and apothecary's assistant, married Margaret Hall in September, 1719. However, he quickly grew tired of her, and hired a gang of ruffians to get rid of her for him, but in the event they failed. So, late at night, on the 17th of October, 1720 he lured her into the King's Park by Holyrood, on the pretext of walking to Duddingston, a small village on the other side of Arthur's Seat. There he murdered her by cutting her throat with a knife, and left her body lying by the wall. Unfortunately for him, he carelessly left some clues behind, and as a result he was in due course convicted of her murder, and hanged in the Grassmarket. A memorial cairn was raised in the King's Park, close to the present day entrance at Willowbrae, to mark the spot where she died.

Arthur's Seat, ye're high an' humpy,
But whit gars ye look sae grumpy?
Perhaps the smeuch o' Aulk Reekie
Maks ye smairt, an' feel richt weerie?

ARTHUR'S SEAT: from the summit of this 822 foot volcanic hill in the centre of the Queen's Park of Holyrood, can be had a spectacular view of Old Edinburgh. Before the days of the Clean Air Act, a pall of smoke from the peat and coal fires down the Royal Mile hung over the town and earned for it the nick-name of "Auld Reekie" (Old Smokie). The name was used in a poem of the 18th century by Robert Fergusson, a fore-runner of Robert Burns, to describe Edinburgh as seen across the Firth of Forth from the Kingdom of Fife.

45 *Young Walter and the Poet*

Professor Ferguson of Sciennes
Kept open-house a lot;
When Robert Burns, the Poet came,
He met young Walter Scott.

Young Walter quietly sat to hear
Whatever might befall;
The Poet spied a print, with lines
He did not know at all.

He wondered who the scene had drawn,
And who the words were by;
"John Langthorne was the poet, Sir,"
Young Walter did reply.

YOUNG WALTER AND THE POET: Adam Ferguson, Professor of
Moral Philosophy at Edinburgh University, frequently held
literary evenings in his home at 7 Sciennes House Place. It was
here in 1786 that a meeting took place between Robert Burns and
the 15 year old Walter Scott. Burns was intrigued by a print of a
young soldier dead in the snow, and asked who had written the
lines printed beneath the picture. Scott was able to remember that
they had been written by a John Langthorne, an 18th century
English poet.

Kirkyard of Greyfriars

In Kirkyard of Greyfriars
Sleep many famous men:
There, two Allan Ramsays,
One good with paint, one pen.

In Kirkyard of Greyfriars
Lie many to be seen:
Master George Buchanan,
Adviser to the Queen.

In Kirkyard of Greyfriars
Rest many famous folk:
The Regent, Earl of Morton,
Deceit his deeds did cloak.

And in this kirkyard also,
The Covenant was signed –
To their old religion
Each themselves would bind.

Memorial to a Surgeon.
Greyfriars Kirkyard.

KIRKYARD OF GREYFRIARS was a burial ground prior to the building of the Old Greyfriars Kirk in 1612. Many distinguished citizens of Old Edinburgh are buried here: Allan Ramsay the Poet (died 1758), Allan Ramsay, his son, the Painter (died 1784), George Buchanan adviser to Mary, Queen of Scots and tutor to her son James VI (died 1582), and James Douglas, Earl of Morton, who was Regent during the minority of James VI, and who was executed by the "Maiden", for his part in the murder of Lord Darnley, in 1580. Also, in 1638, the National Covenant was signed here in the Kirkyard. The Covenant declared the refusal of the Presbyterian church to accept the Episcopalian form of church government being forced on it by Charles I. This protest movement gave rise to the fervid Covenanters who fought for their faith, and were so severely persecuted for this.

Mausoleum of
Sir George Mackenzie.

Kirkyard of
Greyfriars.

ARKN.

47 Sir George Mackenzie

In the Kirkyard of Greyfriars
You will find a mighty tomb,
That of Sir George Mackenzie –
The arbiter of doom
Of all the Covenanters
Who fought at Bothwell Brig;
As Advocate of Scotland
His tomb is very big.
The folk say it is haunted,
So give it a wide berth:
Strong locks on gate and doorway,
His bones deep in the earth.

Boys of the neighbourhood used to dare each
To cry out loudly, when they were in reach:
"Bloody Mackenzie, come oot if ye daur;
Lift up the sneck, and then draw back the bar!"

SIR GEORGE MACKENZIE of Rosenaugh, was Lord Advocate of
Scotland, and the founder of The Advocate's Library. He was seen
as the hated instrument of the English government after his
harsh persecution of the Covenanters captured at the battle of
Bothwell Brig in 1679. 1200 of them, men, women and children,
during the bitter winter of that year, were held captive in the
open, in a corner of Greyfriars Kirkyard. Despite food and
clothing smuggled in for them by sympathetic townsfolk, many of
them died in the extreme conditions. In due course Sir George
himself died, and was buried in a large ornate tomb on the south
side of the same graveyard. It is said to be haunted by his unquiet
spirit, and local boys dare each other to call up his ghost.

48 *Greyfriars Bobby*

Greyfriars Bobby is his name,
A terrier dog, but very tame.
For his master's midday meal
He comes too, but stays at heel.

When his master died, the brave
Dog kept watch upon the grave;
Every day for fourteen years,
Sharp at midday he appears.

Greyfriars Bobby is his name,
Far and wide has gone his fame;
In memory of his loyal trust,
Brodie designed, in bronze, his bust.

GREYFRIARS BOBBY was a little Skye terrier who came with his master, John Gray a Pentland shepherd, each market day into Edinburgh. They would both go into the tavern (now called "Greyfriars Bobby"), opposite to the entrance into that grave-yard, for the midday meal. When his master died in 1858 and was buried on the north side of the kirkyard, the dog kept watch on the grave for fourteen years until 1872. He would cross the street each day to the tavern for food, and then return to his watch. In token of his great loyalty, William Brodie designed a small statue of Bobby which was paid for by Baroness Burdett-Coutts. It is to be found on top of a fountain, opposite to the tavern, at the junction of Candlemaker Row and George IV Bridge.

49 The Witch o' Potterrow

In Sixteen Forty Four, she sell't
Sma' gear tae freend an' foe;
Agnes Finnie was her name,
The Witch o' Potterrow.

She struck folk dumb wha call't her names,
An' brocht folks' fortunes low;
Agnes Finnie was her name,
The Witch o' Potterrow.

She gaed tae court, but lost her cause –
Tae flames she had tae go;
Agnes Finnie was her name,
The Witch o' Potterrow.

THE WITCH O' POTTERROW: in 1644, an elderly woman, Agnes Finnie, lived in the Potterrow, earning a living by selling small articles to whomsoever she could find to buy them. She fell out with her neighbours, and in the ways of the time, she was accused of witchcraft. A woman who miscalled her was said to have been struck dumb as a result; Robert Watt, deacon of the Guild of Cordwainers (shoemakers) got on her wrong side, and thereafter his business failed until he made amends to her, wereupon he prospered once more; when Euphame Kincaid argued with her, Agnes called her a drunkard, and in return she was called a witch. A short while afterwards a heavy beam collapsed and fell on Euphame's daughter, crushing her leg. With such "evidence" against her she was found guilty of witchcraft, and was burned alive at the stake.

50 *Tam o' the Cowgate*

"Tam o' the Cowgate, whaur are ye gaein'
In nicht goon, slippers an' cap?"
"Lads o' the toon a bicker are haein"
So I'll up an' gie them a rap."

Tam o' the Cowgate gied a great laugh,
An' awa tae his bed went he.
"Nae lads o' the toon, or scraichin' riff-raff,
Will e'er get the better o' me!"

TAM O' THE COWGATE was the nickname given by James VI to
Thomas Hamilton of Priestfield, Earl of Melrose, and later 1st
Earl of Haddington. He had been King's Advocate, Lord President
of the Court of Session, and finally Secretary of State in 1612.
There is a story that one night in the Cowgate where he lived, he
went out in his nightgown, slippers and night cap to join in a
street fight between some lads of the town. He took the side of the
High School youths because he had been educated there himself.
Together they successfully chased the opposition into the Grass-
market and out through the West Port where he locked the gate.
The triumphant Tam then retired satisfied to his bed.

51 *The Auld Toon and the New Toon*

Said the Auld Toon tae the New Toon
"Ye're brash, an' think ye're bonnie!"
Said the New Toon tae the Auld Toon
"But style, ye hae nae ony!"

Said the Auld Toon tae the New Toon
"Ye're unco proud an' arty!"
Said the New Toon tae the Auld Toon
"Ye're broken doon an' clarty!"

Said the Auld Toon tae the New Toon
"We maun try tae live taegether."
Said the New Toon tae the Auld Toon
"Then wheesht wi' a' your blether."

The Old Town Skyline.

pwm.

THE AULD TOON AND THE NEW TOON: by the mid 18th century the old historic and largely medieval town of Edinburgh, stretched down the Royal Mile, was bursting at the seams. It had grown filthy and smelly, and there was now a mood in the air for something new. In 1767, the Town Council adopted James Craig's plan for a New Town to be built in the classical style along the ridge of ground immediately to the north of the Nor' Loch. By

1781 St Andrew Square was completed at the east end, and Charlotte Square by 1810 at the west end. It should not, however, be assumed that there was no "new architecture" in the Old Town. The classical style had already been used by John Fergus in 1754 for his development of John Adam's design for the Royal Exchange. George Square had been laid out in 1766 by George and James Brown as the first residential area immediately outside the Old Town limits.

52 *The Philosopher's Dilemma*

David Hume stepped into the mud,
Right up above his knee;
A good wife would not pull him out,
Before "Our Father's" three.

THE PHILOSOPHER'S DILEMMA: David Hume (1711-1776), the Scottish Philosopher and Moralist, was one of the first to move out of the Old Town into the New. There is an apocryphal story that, one night as he was making the crossing, he stepped into the soft mud at the edge of half drained Nor' Loch. He sank right up to his knees. A passing good wife of the town, knowing of his scepticism towards religious practices, insisted that he say the Lord's Prayer and the Creed, before she would help to pull him out. Hume had no choice.

The Mound

'Tween the Auld Toon an' the New Toon
There lies a muckle bog;
The remnant o' the Nor' Loch –
A foul place in the fog!

Some money left on purpose
Built Geordie Boyd's mud brig;
They say twa million cartloads
Of earth they had tae dig!

'Tween the Auld Toon an' the New Toon
Now stands the muckle Mound;
We thank George Boyd, the tailor,
On foot, we cross dry ground!

The Foot of the Mound.

THE MOUND: The Nor' Loch, as part of the Old Town defences, was formed in 1460 by damming the Craig Burn. In order to facilitate a safe passage from the Old Town to the New, it had to be partially drained in 1763, especially to allow for the foundations of the North Bridge. George Boyd, a tailor, left money in his Will for a means to be constructed for crossing the quagmire of the half drained Loch. In 1781, the earth dug up from the foundations of the New Town was gradually built up into a great artificial mound — Geordie Boyd's Mud Brig. By 1783 some 1800 cartloads had been deposited, and by the Mound's completion in 1830, it was estimated to contain some 2 million cartloads of earth.

Each Thursday night, the tale is told,
The Fairy Boy of Leith
Leads out a band of fairy folk,
Upon the Calton heath.

He goes in front, and beats a drum;
He leads them round and round,
Till dancing on, they sink into
A cavern, underground.

Some folk have watched them setting out
Upon their march, until
They suddenly would disappear
Beneath the Calton Hill.

THE FAIRY BOY OF LEITH: the Calton Hill is another volcanic structure, 355 feet high to the north east of the ridge of the Royal Mile. In the 17th century, it was said that every Thursday evening the Fairy Boy of Leith would lead an assorted horde of fairies into an underground cavern below the Calton Hill. He would march in front of them beating a drum, until the moment they would suddenly vanish into the ground, down into the Goblin Halls where elves, goblins, witches, ghosts, demons and fairies gathered for festivities, especially on Hallowe'en, when the revels would last through to the crowing of the first cock at dawn.

55 The Nelson Monument

London has its Nelson's Column;
We his Monument,
Built in form of upright spy-glass
Just as it was meant.

From its top a ball falls slowly
At a steady rate,
So the ships at sea may set their
Naval time-clocks straight.

THE NELSON MONUMENT was designed by Robert Burn in 1816 to commemorate Nelson's victory at Trafalgar on the 21st of October, 1805. Shaped like an inverted telescope, it rises to a height of 102 feet on the top of a rocky outcrop on the southern aspects of the Calton Hill. A spiral staircase of 145 steps leads up to the Observation Platform, above which in 1852 a Time Ball was raised by machinery, to fall down exactly at one o'clock. This was

linked in 1861 by an electrical trigger device to the signal gun fired from the Castle walls at the self-same second. The credulous were led to believe that the Castle gun actually shot down the Time Ball! On the 21st of October each year, the monument carries naval flags which spell out Nelson's famous signal that day — "England expects every man to do his duty."

The Duke of Wellington's Statue

Rearing high, with mounted soldier
Pointing where his troops should wheel,
Sensing battle sits the victor –
The Iron Duke, in bronze, by Steell.

Lately then that field of turmoil
Saw him make the vanquished reel,
Fighting with his forces loyal –
The Iron Duke, in bronze, by Steell.

THE DUKE OF WELLINGTON'S STATUE was designed by Sir John
Steell, and erected in 1852 in front of Robert Adam's Register
House, to commemorate Wellington's victory at Waterloo on the
18th of June, 1815. A wag of the time then making a metallic joke,
referred to it as "The Iron Duke, in bronze by Steell!"

Duke of Wellington's Statue.
MCM.

57 *Princes Street*

A troublesome wind off the Waverley Steps,
Blows all the bonnets about,
And buffets the folk from behind, and in front,
A mischievous blast without doubt.

From the Waverley Steps to the Caley Hotel,
Lies Europe's most elegant street,
With its shops and boutiques, and the view to the south
Of the Old Town, and gaunt Arthur's Seat.

PRINCES STREET: this elegant street was built along the line of a country road called the Lang Dykes on the higher ground to the north of the Old Town. This new street was originally to be called St Giles Street, but George III objected, and it was changed to the Prince's Street, after the Prince Regent (later George IV) and took its present spelling in 1848. It began as a purely residential street on the north side in 1769, but gradually shops were introduced. There was even a plan to build on the south side as well, but that was stopped in order to preserve the spectacular view to the south of the Castle and the ridge of the Old Town running down towards Arthur's Seat. At the east end, the Waverley Steps, leading up from the station, are a notorious windy passage, and at the west end the Caledonian Station Hotel was built in 1904. Hence the saying — "Edinburgh is east windy, and west endy!"

58 *The Scott Monument*

Sir Walter Scott, with dog, sits down
Beneath his Monument;
George Meikle Kemp, the architect
Earned his emolument.

Two hundred feet above the street –
A wedding cake in stone;
With characters from all his books,
Sir Walter sits alone.

THE SCOTT MONUMENT was designed by George Meikle Kemp in 1836. The foundation stone was laid in 1840, and the whole completed in 1844. Sir John Steell provided a statue of Sir Walter Scott (1771-1832), the Scottish novelist and historian, to be placed in the centre of the space at the foot of the gothic structure. It shows Sir Walter sitting with his favourite dog, Maida, at his side. A spiral staircase leads first to a small museum of Scott memorabilia, and then up to the top of the Monument 200 feet above the street. The tower is covered with stone carvings of many of the characters from Scott's novels.

59 *The Three Tall Towers*

Three tall towers stand in a line:
One commemorates, two tell the time;
All three have views; in one you can dine;
One you can live in; two you can climb.

THE THREE TALL TOWERS: the view from the foot of the Mound, looking eastwards along Princes Street, is dominated by three tall towers. The first is the Scott Monument; the second is the clock tower of the North British Hotel (the tower stands 195 feet above the street, with four clock faces, each 13 feet in diameter—the Hotel was opened in 1902); the third is the tower of the Nelson Monument on top of the Calton Hill.

60 The Floral Clock

A clock o' flowers – a braw conceit,
Lying at Allan Ramsay's feet!
Wi' mony a hue frae mony a flower,
An' cuckoo bird tae tell each hour!

THE FLORAL CLOCK is one of the tourist attractions of Edinburgh. It was first laid out in 1903 on a sloping bank at the East entrance to West Princes Street Gardens. It lies at the foot of the statue of Allan Ramsay, the Poet, again by Sir John Steell (1867). The clock is made up of thousands of flowers and plants in a different pattern each year. The hands of the clock are driven by an electrical mechanism, and the hours and quarters are sounded by a cuckoo bird which darts out of a small house.

The Floral Clock.
ARCH.

At one o'clock a gun is fired,
The sudden noise gives quite a fright
As folk at lunch time scurry past –
But they can set their watches right.

At five to one on Calton Hill,
A ball of zinc begins its climb
To fall at stroke of one precise –
So ships at sea can check their time.

TIME CHECKS: the Time Ball on the top of the Nelson Monument is made of zinc, and is 66 inches in diameter. From 1852 it has been raised by machinery, to fall exactly at one o'clock (1300 hours), as a time check for ships at sea. In 1861 it was linked by an electrical device to the Time Gun, fired again at one o'clock from the Castle battlements. This gun gives a fright to visitors if they are not expecting it, but the townsfolk just glance down at their watches to make sure all is in order.

What the Children Know

At midnight, when the sky is dark,
Our statues come alive;
They have a picnic in the park,
And play till half past five.

At midnight, when the moon is out,
Our statues then take care
That no one sees them move about
As they are gathering there.

At midnight, when the city's still,
Our statues hold a race,
But when the dawn creeps up the hill
They must be back in place.

For statues do not sing like larks,
Nor do they eat nor drink,
But elegantly grace our parks –
Or so the adults think!

WHAT THE CHILDREN KNOW: there is an almost universal belief in childhood, that under certain conditions city statues can come alive and get up to all the tricks that children enjoy. This magical moment usually occurs around midnight when there is no adult about to witness what the children know intuitively. There are many statues in Edinburgh — of kings and queens, of soldiers, of statesmen, of men of letters, and of favourite pets — many designed by Sir John Steell, but others by William Brodie, John Hutchinson, William Pomeroy, Birnie Rhind, and Francis Chantrey. Princes Street Gardens would seem to be a central meeting point for all these liberated statue folk!

St Andrew Square is awfu' grand,
Wi' hooses like a palace;
Gin ye are nae sair impressed,
Man, ye maun be callous.

ST ANDREW SQUARE: James Craig in his 1767 plan for the New Town, thought of a central street, George Street after the reigning Monarch George III, balanced by 2 large elegant squares at either end. That in the east was to be called after Scotland's patron saint — Andrew. The first house was built in 1768 by Andrew Crosbie on the east side of the Square. On the site next door, originally earmarked for St Andrew's Church, William Chambers designed a grand palace for Sir Laurence Dundas. This building later became the Excise Office, and then the Royal Bank of Scotland.

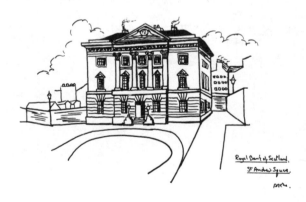

Royal Bank of Scotland,
St Andrew Square,

64 "Saint David"

"Davie, thon's a braw hoose
Ye've biggit o'er the way;
They're callin' it 'St David's Street',
– Ye're canonised today!"

"I like it fine, it suits me best,
It disnae mak me sore;
I think hoo mony a lesser man's
Been made a saint before!"

"SAINT DAVID": the street leading south out off the Square should have been called St Andrew Street, were it not for an "accident". The philosopher David Hume (1711-1776) had 3 homes in the Old Town — in Riddell's Court, in Jack's Land, and in James Court, before he had a fine house built for him in the New Town, in 1771. Knowing his marked anti-clerical views, someone chalked "St David's Street" up on the wall, and so the street has been known ever since. Hume's servant lass rushed in to tell him what had happened, expecting him to be annoyed, but it rather amused him to recall that many a lesser man had been made a saint of, before himself!

65 *Edinburgh Pride*

Charlotte Square
Has its nose in the air,
Its future all before it.

Moray Place
Has an elegant face,
And knows we all adore it.

EDINBURGH PRIDE: the Square at the west end of George Street
was to have been named after England's patron saint — George,
but in deference to the Queen, Charlotte Sophia of Mecklenburg-
Strelitz, it was named Charlotte Square instead. There already
was a George Square, named after the builder, in the Old Town,
and laid out in 1766, but the church in Charlotte Square is still
called St George's! Together with Moray Place, this Square
contains some of the most elegant buildings in the new "Classical"
style.

66 *Charlotte Square and Moray Place*

Said Charlotte Square to Moray Place –
"We have dignity and grace."
Said Moray Place to Charlotte Square –
"We are elegant and fair."

Said Charlotte Square to Moray Place –
"We make use of shade and space."
Said Moray Place to Charlotte Square –
"No wonder people come to stare."

CHARLOTTE SQUARE AND MORAY PLACE are right at the heart of the west end of the New Town. Robert Adam was commissioned to provide a plan and elevation for the north side of Charlotte Square which was begun in 1792, the several individual houses forming an impressive architectural unity. In 1782 the Earl of Moray had bought the oddly shaped land lying between the north side of Charlotte Square and the deep valley of the Water of Leith.

In 1822 his successor to the title advertised the land for development according to a design by James Gillespie, and all the house plots were sold by 1827. Both Charlotte Square and Moray Place have elegant frontages facing onto a central garden, and the delight of these developments lies in the contrast of the lighted facades, and the shady greens.

67 *Lighting-up Times*

Link-boy, link-boy, bring your light,
Disperse the shadows of this night;
Link-boy, link-boy, here's the horn,
We'll sleep safe till light of morn.

Leerie, Leerie, light our lamp,
As the New Town streets you tramp;
Leerie, Leerie, home to bed,
Night and day will soon be wed.

LIGHTING-UP TIMES: from the end of the 15th century onwards, the citizens of Edinburgh had to carry lights for their own safety, and lanterns were hung in the streets from 1554. By 1557, no one was allowed in the streets after dark without a light because of the level of street crime. In 1653, it was decreed that lanterns must be hung outside houses from 5 pm until curfew. The Town Council passed an Act for the lighting of the New Town in 1785, but it was not until 1817 that the Edinburgh Gas Company was formed, and gas used for public lighting of shops and streets. Electric lighting eventually came in around 1895.

LINK-BOYS were youths who plied for hire, and with lighted torches would conduct citizens about the streets after dark. They extinguished their torches at day break in link-horns, which can still be seen on the public railings in Charlotte Square.

LEERIE THE LAMPLIGHTER is a character in Stevenson's *Child's Garden of Verses*. There was a gas lamp outside 17 Heriot Row where the young Louis lived. He would watch for Leerie every night before the lonely child went off to bed. "For we are very lucky, with a lamp before the door ...".

68 *The Dean Bridge*

The Dean Bridge is terribly tall,
Please take care that you do not fall
Down into the Water of Leith
Far below, as it flows beneath.

THE DEAN BRIDGE was built in 1832, to a design by Thomas Telford, across the deep ravine of the Water of Leith. The roadway is 106 feet above the Dean Valley below. The bridge connects the West End with the properties laid out on the lands of the estate of Learmonth, Lord Provost of the time. The bridge was erected almost entirely at his own expense. Because of its uninterrupted height, the bridge has been used by suicides leaping from the parapet.

69 The Water of Leith

The Water of Leith
Rises up from a heath,
In the heart of the far Pentland Hills.

It flows bright and clean
Past the Village of Dean,
And the foot of the old Canon Mills.

THE WATER OF LEITH rises on the northern slopes of Craigengar (1700 feet) in the Pentland Hills. In 1793, it passed some 80 mills on the 10 mile stretch on either side of Balerno. It flows through the Village of Dean (originally the Village of Water of Leith, the ford here being the main entry into the town from the west) then on through Stockbridge to Canonmills, to its final outlet in Leith Harbour, some 25 miles from its source.

70 St Bernard's Well

St Bernard's Well
Stands in a dell,
Surrounded by beautiful trees;
Sick folk do think
Its waters to drink
In the hope of curing disease.

ST BERNARD'S WELL: in a leafy dell of the Dean Valley, a healing spring was discovered in 1760. An ornate classical structure was erected over this spring by Lord Gardenstone (him of the pig) in 1788, to a design of Alexander Nasmyth. It resembled the Temple of Tivoli in Italy, and contained a statue of Hygeia, the Goddess of Health. The whole structure was renovated in 1887 by Thomas Nelson, the printer.

71 *The Crazy Balloonist*

Up in a balloon, and far, far away
Soaring above us, the mad Lunardi;
Down thro' the clouds to land loudly in Fife,
Such a performance might win him a wife!

THE CRAZY BALLOONIST: on 5th October, 1785 some two years
after the Mongolfier brothers' first successful ascent in a hot air
balloon in France, the Italian balloonist Vincenzo Lunardi made a
historic ascent from the gardens of George Heriot's Hospital. He
sailed majestically over the New Town as the prevailing winds
carried him north-east across the Forth. He then descended down
through the clouds, blowing loudly on a trumpet, to land in a field
near Ceres in Fife. A group of farm workers thought this must
herald the end of the world! Thereafter, Lunardi became a great
favourite with the ladies, and he was given the Freedom of the
City as befits the first man to have flown over it.

The statue folk survey the town,
Alert by night and day;
They watch us, steadfastly and still,
As we pass on our way.

I wish I knew if they can feel,
And wonder what each thinks;
If I creep up so quiet, might I
Catch them in forty winks?

CITY STATUES: most of Edinburgh's statues are to be found in the New Town. There are many to be found in the gardens on the south side of Princes Street. Others stand strategically, at the crossings of the main streets on George Street. Others stand majestically in the centre of the ornate gardens of James Craig's New Town squares and places. They form a whole population, but the child wonders if they can feel like us, what do they think about, and are there times when we might catch them nodding off?

"Where are you sailing to, my little lad,
All on this long summer's day?"
"I'm sailing for Spain and the Barbary Main,
For China, and lands far away."

"How will you steer there, my brave little lad,
All on this tempest tossed sea?"
"I'll steer by the light of the stars shining bright,
And then I'll be back home for tea."

"When will you reach there, my hopeful young lad,
So far to the back of beyond?"
"I'll reach there today, if you'll take me to play
Down beside Inverleith Pond."

INVERLEITH POND: from the child's viewpoint, Edinburgh is well served with ponds and lochs — Blackford Pond, Duddingston Loch, Dunsappie Loch, St Margaret's Loch, Lochend Loch, Inverleith Pond, as well as the historic and now drained Nor' Loch. Some of them are artificial; others are the result of the excavating power of the glaciers of the Ice Age coming up against a number of volcanic plugs. Inverleith Pond, in the public park just west of the Botanic Gardens, is a favourite site for the sailing of model yachts. There, many a historic voyage has begun, only to end in tragedy, as a yacht heels over and cannot right itself, or disappears quickly out of reach in the grasp of a perverse wind.

74 *The Warlock o' Merchiston*

John Napier o' Merchiston
Bides in his Tower,
Devisin' his Logarithms
Wi' uncanny power.

John Napier o' Merchiston,
A cockerel on his airm,
Kens a' by his secret airts,
But comes tae nae hairm.

THE WARLOCK O' MERCHISTON: John Napier of Merchiston Castle (1550-1617) first went to St Andrews University, and then to Italy where he studied the science of mathematics. He returned to Edinburgh, where in 1614 he published his system of Logarithms, dedicated to the monarch. People thought that he must be a magician because of his mathematical powers, and his wit. Stories began circulating that he had been seen with a black cockerel, (obviously a familiar), on his shoulder. Despite these rumours and the superstition of the time, he avoided any charges of witchcraft, and died a respected academic in 1617.

A braw Italian wi' the King,
Said aince that he would fly
Wi' wings o' feathers, frae the wa's
O' ony castle high.

The King, he thocht tae test the case,
An' chose the fatefu' day;
Oor mannie ordered wings be made –
He'd manage, come whit may.

He jumpit aff in guid array,
But drappit like a stane;
He hit the groun' wi' awfu' dunt,
An' brakit his thigh bane.

"Wi' feathers gat frae hens," he claimed,
"Yon wings jist wudnae rise;
Ye ken thae birds the midden seek,
An' no' the bricht blue skies!"

A FLIGHT O' FANCY: James IV (1488-1513) was something of a renaissance prince. He was well versed in the arts, with a great interest in science and invention. He was fond of sport — he played golf and tennis, he fished and went after wild fowl. He raced horses and took part in tournaments. He commissioned the Great Michael, the greatest ship that Scotland had ever seen, and denuded Fife of its trees in the process! He founded the College of Surgeons and Barbers in 1505. He was a true experimenter — he marooned a child with a dumb woman on the Bass Rock to see if the child would develop any spontaneous speech of its own. He was thus greatly intrigued when an Italian cleric claimed he would fly by means of a pair of artificial wings from the high walls of any of the King's castles. In the event he singularly failed, and blamed this on the number of hens' feathers that had been put into the wings! Tradition has it that this event occurred at Stirling Castle, one of the King's royal residences, but it could equally have happened at Edinburgh.

76 *The Twa Burghs*

"Musselburgh was a burgh when Edinburgh was nane;
Musselburgh will be a burgh when Edinburgh is gane."
"Edinburgh and Musselburgh, royal burghs apiece,
Edinburgh and Musselburgh, bide ye in peace."

THE TWA BURGHS: There has always been a strong rivalry between Edinburgh and Musselburgh its near neighbour, each being royal burghs. Edinburgh received its royal charter in 1329 from Robert the Bruce. Musselburgh traces its origins back to Roman times, and although it did not receive its charter until 1632, it had been a "burgh of regality" for centuries before.

77 *Musselburgh, Fisherrow*

Musselburgh, Fisherrow,
Tell me where the lilies grow.

By the River Esk and bridge,
By St Michael's on the ridge;
By Inveresk where Romans camped,
By tracks where ancient Britons tramped;
By paper mills, and Bruntons works,
There the Arum Lily lurks.

Musselburgh, Fisherrow,
I know where the lilies grow.

MUSSELBURGH, FISHERROW: Musselburgh, Fisherrow and Inveresk, now all part of the same urban development, were famous each in their own right. Musselburgh, on the River Esk, for its medieval bridge built on Roman foundations, the Chapel of

Loretto, the Links where James IV played golf in 1504, and now its paper mills and Bruntons wire works; Fisherrow for its harbour, its fishing fleet and its fisherwives in their traditional costume; Inveresk with its Roman settlement, and the Kirk of St Michael an early 19th century lineal descendant of ancient places of worship since the first days of Christianity in SE Scotland. Here, in the 18th century the Rev. Alexander "Jupiter" Carlyle was minister for 57 years, described by Sir Walter Scott as "the grandest demigod" he ever saw. There is a walk by the banks of the Esk between Musselburgh and Inveresk, where wild garlic and Arum Lilies used to grow.

78 *The Hills of Home*

Of Pentland days and Pentland ways
Full many a song is sung;
Caerketton's crags and Allermuir
Delight the poet's tongue.

West Linton leads by Cauldstane Slap
Across to Harperrig,
And Carlops crouches close beneath
The Kips, by North Esk brig.

By Flotterstone to wild Glen Corse,
And Scald Law tops we roam;
From Hillend Park to Nine Mile Burn,
Across our Hills of Home.

THE HILLS OF HOME was the affectionate name given to the Pentlands by Robert Louis Stevenson. He spent many a happy day in Swanston Cottage, close by the small shepherd's clachan of thatched cottages tucked in beneath the northern slopes of Caerketton and Allermuir. The Pentland range, with Scald Law (1898 feet) its highest point, runs some 25 miles north-east to south-west from the western edge of the city of Edinburgh. In fact, Hillend Park with its ski-slope, is now just within the city boundary. The hills and the hidden valleys in between, such as Glencorse, provide a haven of peace even though they come to within 5 miles of the city centre. The origin of the name Pentlands is obscure, but it may be a corruption of "Pictlands", and certainly on the south-east slopes of Castlelaw Hill, there is on the 900 foot contour, an Iron Age ring fort, containing within it a souterrain or earth house such as the Picts might use. Safe within a fold of the foothills is Old Glencorse Kirk with its "clinkum clank o' Sabbath bells". In a letter to S.R. Crockett, Stevenson asks if he knows "where the road crosses the burn under Glencorse Church". He should go there and say a prayer for him. "See that it's a sunny day. I would like it to be a Sunday". Stevenson died aged 44 years in Samoa in 1894, and never saw his beloved Pentlands again. For many an exiled Scot, Edinburgh is the outline of the Old Town seen against the evening sky, and the gentle slopes of the Hills of Home to the south.

Time Scale

EDWIN OF NORTHUMBRIA

c.629   Building of the first fortress at Edinburgh.

MALCOLM II (1005-1034)

1018   After Carham, Edinburgh Castle becomes Scottish.

MALCOLM III (1057-1093)

1068   Margaret Atheling comes to Scotland
1093   Deaths of Margaret, and Malcolm Canmore.

DAVID I (1124-1153)

1124   Edinburgh Castle becomes permanent royal residence.
1128   Founding of the Abbey of the Holy Rood.

ROBERT I (1306-1329)

1314   Sir Thomas Randolph captures the Castle.
1329   Bruce gives Royal Charter to Edinburgh.

JAMES III (1460-1488)

1460   Nor' Loch formed for defence.

JAMES IV (1488-1513)

1498   First plans for Holyrood Palace.
1505   Founding of the College of Surgeons and Barbers.

JAMES V (1513-1542)

1520   "Cleanse the Causeway".

MARY (1542-1567)

1566   Death of David Riccio
1567   Explosion at Kirk o'Field

JAMES VI (1567-1625)

1580   Execution of Regent Morton
1590   Burning of the Witches on Castle Hill.
1595   Shooting of Bailie MacMorran.
1612   Tam o' the Cowgate made Secretary of State.

1614 Napier publishes his system of Logarithms.

CHARLES I (1625-1649)

1637 Jenny Geddes and the St Giles riots
1638 Signing of the National Covenant.
1644 Burning of the Witch of Potterrow.

THE COMMONWEALTH (1649-1660)

1650 Execution of the Marquis of Montrose.
George Heriot's Hospital

CHARLES II (1660-1685)

Execution of the Marquis of Argyll.
1685 Equestrian Statue to Charles II.

GEORGE I (1714-1727)

1720 Nichol Muschat murders his wife.
1724 Half Hangit Maggie Dickson.

GEORGE II (1727-1760)

1730 "Gardy Loo" repressed.
1736 Porteous Riots.
1753 Building of John Adam's Royal Exchange.
1758 Death of Allan Ramsay the Poet
1759 Death of Countess Lady Stair

GEORGE III (1760-1820)

1767 Adoption of James Craig's plan for the New Town
1817 Founding of the Edinburgh Gas Company.

GEORGE IV (1820-1830)

1820 Construction of the Radical Road.
1829 Hanging of William Burke.
      Return of Mons Meg to Edinburgh from London.

WILLIAM IV (1830-1837)

1832 Construction of the Dean Bridge.

VICTORIA (1837-1901)

1844 Erection of the Scott Monument.

1847   Guthrie's first Ragged School.
1855   Camera Obscura in Short's Observatory.
1861   Collapse of Heave Awa' House.
1870   Completion of the Mound.
1872   Death of Greyfriars Bobby.
1895   Installation of electric street lighting.

EDWARD VII (1901-1910)

1903   Construction of the Floral Clock.

Scots (Lallans) Glossary

A' — all
Aboot — about
Aff — off
Agin — against
Aiblins — perhaps, possibly
Ain — own
Airms — arms
Airts — skill, knowledge
An' — and
Ane — one
Anither — another
A'taegither — altogether
Auld — old
Awa' — away
Awfu' — awful
Aye — always, ever

Bairnie — little child
Bane — bone
Bicker — quarrel
Bide — to remain, live in, await
Biggit — built
Blether — chatter
Bonnie — attractive, pretty
Brae — hill, slope
Brakit — broke
Braw — fine, pleasant,
  handsome
Bricht — bright
Brig — bridge
Brocht — brought
Buiks — books
Buryin' kist — coffin

Cairt — cart
Callit — called, summoned
Cam' — came
Clankit — clanked
Clarty — dirty, filthy, muddy

Clavers — gossip
Clink — prison, gaol
Cloot — blow, struck
Corp — dead body
Crack — chat
Cronies — pals, friends,
  associates
Cuddie — donkey, poor type
  horse

Dae — to do, act
Daunce — to dance
Daur — to dare
Deave — to deafen
Deid — dead
Dinna — do not
Disna — does not
Doon — down
Drappit — dropped
Dunt — blow, heavy fall

E'er — ever, before

Faither — father
Fell — grim, dark
Frae — from
Freend — friend
Fricht — fright
Frichtsome — frightful
Freend — friend
Fu' — full

Gaes — goes
Gane — gone
Gangs — goes
Gart — made
Gat — got
Gear — goods, objects
Ghaisties — ghosts

99

Gied — gave
Girn — to grouse, complain
Gif — if
Gin — if, whether
Greet — to cry, weep
Guid — good

Hae — have
Haill — whole
Hairm — harm
Hairty — hearty
Hangit — hanged
Hauf — half
Heicht — height
Heid — head
Hoo — how
Hoose — house
Hunkered doon — crouching
  down

I' — in
Ilka — each

Jouked — dodged, swerved

Ken — to know
Kenn'd — knew, known
Kenspeckle — conspicuous,
  recognisable
Kin — can
Kirk — church
Kist — chest, coffin

Lang — long
Lang syne — long ago, long
  since
Leid — lead

Mak' — to make
Mair — more
Maun — must

Merks — marks
Midden — refuse dump
Mirk — gloom, darkness
Moose — mouse
Mou' — mouth
Muckle — big, great

Nae — no
Nane — none
Nicht — night
Noo — now

O'er — over
Objeckit — objected
Ony — any
Oot — out

Perhaips — perhaps

Reekie — smoky
Richt — right
Richteous — righteous
Roond — round
Roun' — round
Rowt — riot, tumult
Runner — gutter

Sair — sore
Schule — school
Scraitchin' — screeching
Scunner — disgust, nausea
Searchit — searched
Seekit — sought
Shooglin' — shaking
Sic — such
Sichts — sights
Siller — silver
Skulk — to lurk, sneak
Sma' — small
Smairt — smart
Smeuch — smoke

Sneck — latch of a door or gate
Snug — warm and comfortable
Snuggit — nestled
Sodgers — soldiers
Soun' — sound
Squint — to look sideways at
Spak' — spoke
Stane — stone
Stauns — stands
Sune — soon

Taen — taken
Tak — took
Tapsalteerie — topsy-turvy, upside down
Thae — those, these
Thair — there, their
Thocht — thought, decided
Thon — those, that
Tirled — rattled the door latch
Toun — town
Twa — two

Unco — rather, extremely

Wa' — wall
Warld — world
Waur — worse
Weerie — weary
Wha — who
Whaur — where
Wheest — be quiet!
Whigmaleerie — foolish fancy
Wi' — with
Wight — fellow, person
Windae — window
Worrit — strangled
Wudnae — would not

Yanked — jerked
Ye — you
Yer — your
Yett — gate
Yon — that, those

Background Sources

J. F. Birrell (1980). *An Edinburgh Alphabet*. James Thin, Edinburgh.

Charles W. Cameron (1975). *Curiosities of Old Edinburgh*. Albyn Press, Edinburgh.

E. F. Catford (1975). *Edinburgh: story of a city*. Hutchinson, London.

Robert Chambers (1868). *Traditions of Edinburgh*. W&R. Chambers, Edinburgh.

David Daiches (1978). *Edinburgh*. Panther Books, Granada, London.

Owen Dudley Edwards. *Burke and Hare*. Polygon Books, EUSPB, Edinburgh.

Duncan Fraser (1976). *Edinburgh in Olden Times*. Standard Press, Montrose.

James Grant (1883). *Old and New Edinburgh*, Vol 1-3. Cassell and Co., London.

P. Hume Brown (1907). *History of Scotland*, Vol 1-2. Oliver and Boyd, Edinburgh.

Charles McKean. *Edinburgh, an Illustrated Architectural Guide*. RIAS Publications, Edinburgh

Moray McLaren (1965). *Shell Guide to Scotland*. Ebury Press, London.

H. W. Meikle (1947). *Scotland*. Thomas Nelson, Edinburgh.

Andrew Pennycook (1973). *Literary and Artistic Landmarks of Edinburgh*. Albyn Press, Edinburgh.

John Prebble (1971). *The Lion in the North*. Secker and Warburg, London.

E. B. Simpson (1912). *The R. L. Stevenson Originals*. T. N. Foulis, Edinburgh.

R. L. Stevenson (1896)(1973). *Weir of Hermiston*. Holmes McDougall, London.

George Malcolm Thomson (1967). *The Crime of Mary Stuart*. Hutchinson, London.

Alexander Warrack (1952). *Scots Dictionary*. W & R. Chambers, Edinburgh.

Index

(References are to title numbers and not to page numbers)

104